SCIENCE ENCYCLOPEDIA

SCIENTISTS,
LAWS AND
CHEMICAL REACTIONS

Om
KIDZ
An imprint of Om Books International

Contents

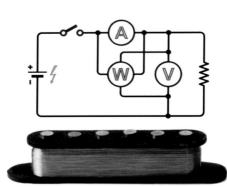

SCIENTISTS

Humans have progressed immensely over the last centuries. This has been accomplished by the great contributions of some people in the field of science. These great scientists have made amazing inventions and discoveries that transformed our lives. Galileo made outstanding discoveries in the fields of physics and astronomy. Charles Darwin illustrated the theory of evolution. Archimedes was responsible for laying the foundation of calculus. Thomas Edison created 1093 inventions, including light, power, battery, telegraph and mining. Sir Isaac Newton discovered the laws of motion, studied sound and invented the telescope.

Famous Physicists

There have been a large number of world-renowned physicists who have made many useful contributions to the field of physics. Some of the popular ones are mentioned below.

Galileo Galilei

Galileo (1564–1642) was an Italian mathematician, physicist, astronomer, engineer and philosopher who played a key role in the scientific revolution during the time of the Renaissance. He discovered the telescopic confirmation of the phases of Venus and discovered four large satellites of the Jupiter and analysed sunspots. His work in applied science has been noteworthy with his invention of the thermometer. His contributions for the betterment of the working of telescope and compass is incredible.

Galileo thermometer.

FUN FACT

Albert Einstein's favourite scientist was Galilei Galileo.

As a child, Einstein was very slow at learning and learnt to speak very late.

Sir Isaac Newton

Isaac Newton (1642–1727), was an English scientist, mathematician and physicist. He proposed many path breaking theories at the age of 23 years.

His curiosity and inquisitive nature led him to develop his theories of gravitation that in turn, helped him to generate the Newton's Laws of Motion.

The famous principles by Sir Isaac Newton have been instrumental in formulating the laws of motion and the universal knowledge of gravitation as a force. He is also well-known for his invention of the reflecting telescope and developing a theory of the colour based spectrum of a prism. Sir Isaac Newton has been a renowned and key figure in the scientific revolution over the years. His foundation theories of classical mechanics, creditable role in the development of calculus and various contributions to the field of optics have been noteworthy.

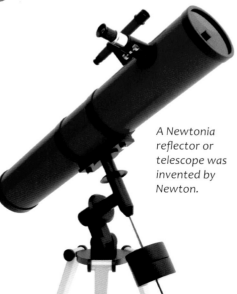

A Newtonia reflector or telescope was invented by Newton.

Orbit of Earth around the Sun.

Gravity or gravitation is a natural process by which physical bodies attract one another. Gravity provides weight to the physical objects and directs them to fall towards the ground if dropped. In modern physics, gravitation is accurately described as the consequence of space-time. For most situations, gravity is approximated by Newton's law of universal gravitation, which considers that the gravitational force of the mass of two bodies will increase if the product of the masses increases and vice versa; and will decrease if the square of the distance between them increases and vice versa.

be much greater than, say, an apple. That is why the apple moves towards Earth. On the other hand, the mass of the Sun is much larger than that of Earth and so Earth rotates around the Sun rather than the other way round.

Also, gravity is everywhere. We might feel that there is no gravity in space, but gravity is present even in space. However, because it is very far away from any object having mass, the gravity there is weak. The force of gravity that an object with mass exerts on another object weakens as the distance between the two object increases.

Application

When an object falls to Earth, not only is Earth attracting that object towards itself, but the object is pulling Earth towards itself as well. However, if we compare the masses of the object falling to Earth and Earth itself, the mass of Earth will

Newton's Universal Law of Gravitation

$$F_G = \frac{Gm_E m_M}{r_{EM}^2}$$

g

The moon's gravitational field is causing the Earth to accelerate towards the moon

Moon

a_M

r_M

V

$$F_{EM} = -F_{ME}$$

Newton's Third Law

Earth

R_E

The Earth's gravitational field is causing the moon to accelerate towards the Earth

Universal gravitation equation

Newton's law of universal gravitation extends gravity beyond Earth and describes the universality of gravity. This is because all objects attract each other with the force of gravitational attraction.

This is mathematically represented as,

$$F = \frac{Gm_1 m_2}{r^2}$$

where, "F" stands for the gravitational force of attraction, "m_1 and m_2" are the two masses, "r" is the distance between the two masses and "G" is the universal gravitational constant.

FUN FACT

If you weigh 150 pounds on Earth, you would weigh about 354 pounds on Jupiter while on Mars you would merely weigh 9 pounds because Mars's gravity is lower than that of Earth.

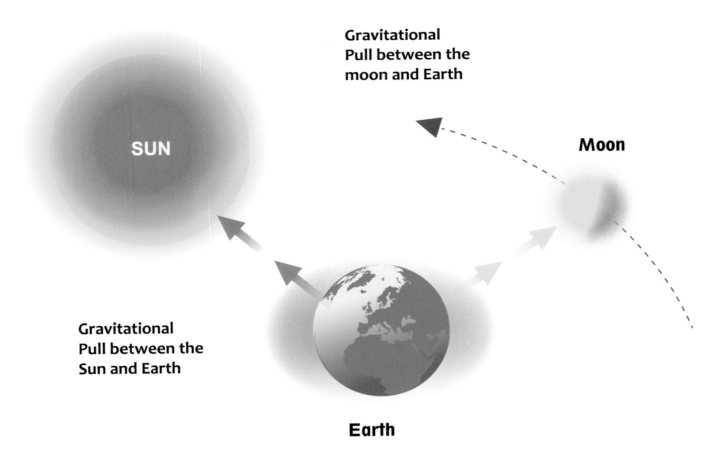

**Gravitational
Pull between the
moon and Earth**

SUN

Moon

**Gravitational
Pull between the
Sun and Earth**

Earth

Time and tide

We know about Earth's gravitational force on the moon because of which it rotates around Earth and does not simply float away into space. But did you know that the moon also exerts a gravitational pull on Earth? This is why we experience tides. The area of Earth that is faced by the moon experiences a high tide as the water gets pulled towards it. Similarly, the areas not facing the moon experience a low tide. This is a very good example of Newton's law of universal gravitation.

On the other hand, the Sun too has an effect on the tides of Earth. However, the Sun's tidal effect on Earth is not very prominently visible as it is so far away from Earth. This proves that the larger the distance between the two objects, the weaker the gravity.

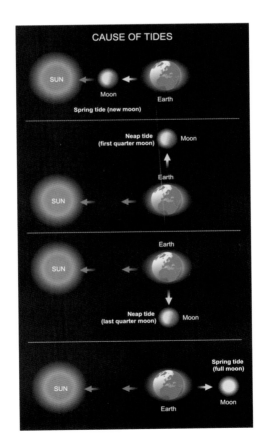

CAUSE OF TIDES

SUN ← Moon ← Earth
Spring tide (new moon)

Neap tide
(first quarter moon) Moon

Earth

SUN ← ←

Earth

SUN ← ←

Neap tide
(last quarter moon) Moon

SUN ← ← Earth → Spring tide
(full moon)
Moon

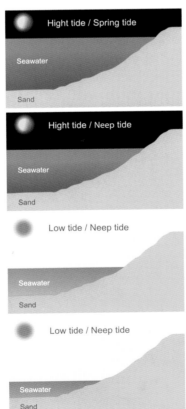

Hight tide / Spring tide
Seawater
Sand

Hight tide / Neep tide
Seawater
Sand

Low tide / Neep tide
Seawater
Sand

Low tide / Neep tide
Seawater
Sand

Ohm's Law

Ohm's law relates current, voltage and resistance, which are the three basic quantities of electricity. Hence, this is considered as the most basic law of electrical engineering.

What is Ohm's Law?

Ohm's law states that the current flowing through a conductor is directly proportional to the potential difference across its two points. By naming the proportionality constant as R in this equation, we will get,

$$I = \frac{V}{R}$$

where, I = current flowing, V = potential difference, R = Resistance

This is Ohm's law.

Resistance came to be measured in ohms after the name of its discoverer. In 1827, German physicist Georg Simon Ohm described how applied voltage and current are mathematically related through simple electrical circuits using different lengths of wire. This law was then modified by Gustav Kirchhoff to determine the conductivity of a conductor.

$$J = \sigma E$$

where, J = current density in a resistive material, E = electric field, σ (Sigma) = conductivity

Ohm's law is an empirical equation. It has a broad area of scope from a wide range of length scales , which can work even for silicon wires that are four atoms wide. Materials that obey Ohm's law are called Ohmic or linear. This law can be used to solve simple circuits and for calculating the EMF, that is, the electromotive force of a cell. By applying Ohm's law, we can find out the value of resistance in a circuit, by knowing only the values of the current flowing and the potential difference in a circuit.

The circuit shows the relationship between current, voltage and the resistance, following the Ohm's law.

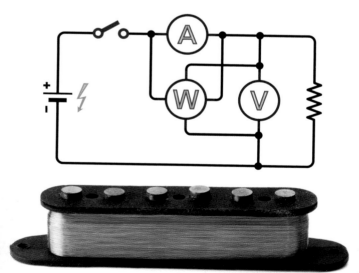

Molecular explanation

At the molecular level, a solid conductor contains free electrons that carry negative charge. The atoms and ions are heavier in weight as compared to electrons. Therefore, they do not contribute towards the flow of the current and become barriers to the path of electron flow. These barriers create resistance in a circuit. When we apply a voltage, V, between the leads of a resistor, we can expect a current, I = V/R, to flow through it. The electrons keep being accelerated by the applied static electric field or voltage. Thus, they acquire some kinetic energy as they move towards the positive end of the piece of material (resistor). However, before moving away, they collide with an atom or ion and lose some of their kinetic energy and bounce back. Due to the presence of a static electric field, the free electrons accelerate again. This method of drifting or diffusing electrons in the presence of static atoms and ions is the simple physics behind Ohm's law.

Space Law

Since humans are now capable of entering space and have access to it, it becomes necessary that some rules and laws are put in place to protect space as well as themselves. Care needs to be taken that this access is not misused.

How it began

The conduct in the area above Earth as well as the lower atmosphere is regulated by the international law and is known as the space law. In 1957, US President Eisenhower proposed this concept to the UN with regards to the disarmament negotiation. After the launch of the Russian satellite Sputnik in 1957 and the US satellite Explorer 1, both the countries took the initiative to put these international space laws in place.

Peaceful exploration

As the world stands right now, if any country is to find any unexplored, uninhabited land, they can legally claim it as a part of their country. However, when it comes to space, this rule cannot be applied. The space right above a particular country cannot be considered as a part of that country, neither can any unexplored space territory can be claimed by that country. All the countries have the permission to peacefully explore space.

Ban of nuclear testing

A permanent Outer Space Committee was formed in 1959. When the intention to carry out nuclear tests in space became evident, this committee signed a treaty to prohibit it. The Nuclear Test Ban Treaty was signed in 1963.

FUN FACT

There is a Moon Treaty that prohibits countries from exploiting its and other celestial bodies' resources. However, this treaty has not been ratified yet.

Ohm's Law

As seen, the presence of weapons in space gives a sizable tactical and strategic advantage to the party that holds them. Mutually Assured Destruction (MAD) would then trigger an arms race in space. So, as MAD became the deterrent strategy between the two superpowers during the Cold War, many countries worked together to avoid extending the threat of nuclear weapons to space based launchers to prevent this catastrophe.

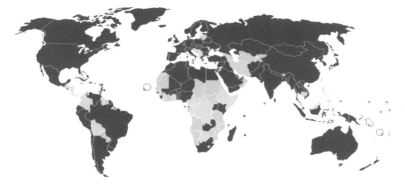

The map shows the stance of each country on the Outer Space Treaty. The nations in green have signed and ratified the treaty and the ones in yellow have signed it, but not ratified it. The ones in grey have not signed the treaty.

The Outer Space Treaty

The Outer Space Treaty is currently agreed to by a majority of the World's Nation states. The Legal Subcommittee of the United Nations General Assembly (UNGA) originally formed it in 1966. Later that year, the UNGA voted to accept the treaty through a majority.

Provisions of the Outer Space Treaty

The principles of the Outer Space Treaty are given below:

● The exploration and use of outer space shall be carried out for the benefit and in the interests of all countries and shall be the province of all humankind.

● Outer space shall be free for exploration and use by all states.

● Outer space is not subject to national appropriation by claim of sovereignty, by means of use or occupation or by any other means.

● States shall not place nuclear weapons or other weapons of mass destruction in orbit or on celestial bodies or station them in outer space in any other manner.

● The moon and other celestial bodies shall be used exclusively for peaceful and non-military purposes.

● Astronauts shall be regarded as the envoys of humankind.

● States shall be responsible for national space activities whether carried out by governmental or non-governmental activities.

● States shall be liable for damage caused by their space objects.

● States shall avoid harmful contamination of space and celestial bodies.

Shortcomings of this treaty

An artists' representation of Earth and the space in future. ▼

The outer space treaty does not ban the placement of weapons in space in general, but only nuclear weapons and weapons of mass destruction. Thus, in 2006, the UN General Assembly proposed The Space Preservation Treaty against all weapons.

CHEMICAL
REACTIONS

The atom is the smallest unit that any element is made up of. A bunch of atoms is called molecules. Transformation of molecules from one form to another is called a chemical reaction. A chemical reaction occurs when two different molecules of two different elements interact with each other. The bonding forces that bind two atoms are broken and new bonding forces are created, resulting in the formation of a whole new compound having totally different properties as compared to the substances with which it was originally made up.

Endothermic Reaction

The reactions that absorb heat or energy from their surroundings are called endothermic reactions. When they absorb heat from the surrounding, the surrounding temperature decreases. A simple example of endothermic reactions is the process of photosynthesis. This is where plants prepare their own food by taking in atmospheric carbon dioxide and giving out oxygen. This not only creates oxygen for everyone but also brings a drop in the temperature of the surroundings.

Basic principle

The process of photosynthesis requires heat and light energy from the Sun. It is said that we must not go near plants during the night as they release carbon dioxide, which is harmful for human beings. The binding forces between two atoms of an element or compound is so strong that they cannot be easily broken, so during a chemical reaction, they absorb heat energy that breaks the bonding forces and forms new products. Endothermic reactions are not spontaneous reactions. Work needs to be done for these types of reactions.

In endothermic reactions, the change in the temperature of products is much higher than the reactants. That is why they absorb heat. Enthalpies of both products and reactants are greater than zero.

Application

When it is very hot and the Sun shines brightly, we see that the water from lakes and ponds begins to evaporate. When this happens, the water is actually absorbing the heat from the environment in order to bring about the evaporation of water. That is the reason why the hotter the days, the cooler are the nights. The water vapour in air contributes to the temperature drop as well.

Water evaporation.

Melting of ice.

Endothermic reaction formula

A system of reactants that absorbs heat from the surroundings in an endothermic reaction causes cooling as the heat in the products is higher than the heat in the reactants of the system.

$N_2(g) + O_2(g) = 2NO(g)$ $\quad(\Delta H = +180.5\ kJ > 0)$

$C(s) + 2S(s) = CS_2(l)$ $\quad\quad(\Delta H = +92.0\ kJ > 0)$

As the enthalpies of these reactions are greater than zero, they are endothermic reactions.

Exothermic Reaction

When a chemical reaction between two substances occurs, energy is released in the form of light, heat, sound or electricity. When large amounts of heat or energy are released after a chemical reaction, such reactions are called exothermic reactions. As exothermic reactions release heat, they raise the temperature of the surroundings around them.

What is an exothermic reaction?

An exothermic reaction is any reaction that releases energy during chemical reactions. The word exothermic can be broken into "exo", which means to exit, and "therm", which means heat. The opposite of an exothermic reaction is an endothermic one, where "endo" means to absorb or let in. In an exothermic reaction, the energy released can be in multiple forms, including heat, light, sound or electricity. This is because when old bonds of the reactants are broken in exothermic reactions, they hold the two atoms together and energy is released in different forms. Based on the reactants that are involved, the heat released can be more or less; however, there will be a certain output of energy for certain.

Exothermic reactions

Exothermic and endothermic reactions result in energy level differences and thereby differences in heat (ΔH), the sum of all potential and kinetic energies. ΔH is calculated by the system, not the surrounding environment in a reaction. A system that releases heat to the surroundings has a negative ΔH by convention as the enthalpy of the products is lower than the enthalpy of the reactants of the system.

$C(s) + O_2(g) = CO_2(g)$ ($\Delta H = -393.5$ kJ)

$H_2(g) + 1/2\ O_2(g) = H_2O(l)$ ($\Delta H = -285.8$ kJ)

The enthalpies of these reactions are less than zero and are therefore exothermic reactions. For example, when a nail rusts, heat is released into the surroundings.

Rusting nails.

Snowing, precipitation.

Kinetics of Reaction

Chemical kinetics is taking into consideration the rate of the reaction. It is defined as the study of the rate at which a chemical reaction occurs. As it examines how different conditions affect a chemical reaction, it can also be called reaction kinetics. The speed at which products are formed in a chemical reaction is affected by many factors like temperature of the surroundings, catalyst and air pressure.

Adding salt to ice helps it to melt faster.

Rate of reactions

Rate of reactions is the rate of change in concentrations or the amount of either reactants or products. With respect to reaction rates, we may deal with average rates, instantaneous rates or initial rates depending on the experimental conditions. Thermodynamics and kinetics are two major factors that influence reaction rates. The study of energy gained or released in chemical reactions is called thermodynamics. However, thermodynamic data has no direct correlation with reaction rates, for which the kinetic factor is perhaps more important.

Factors affecting kinetics

The rate of reaction is the rate at which the concentrations of reactants and products change. Catalysts play a very important role in determining the speed of the reactions. These are the substances which help in completing the reaction faster. By introducing a catalyst, the rate of reaction increases. Furthermore, temperature acts as a catalyst. Higher the temperature, the faster is the rate of reaction.

Hydrochloric acid (HCl)

Hydrochloric acid is a strong acid. It ionises almost completely in water. It is colourless in appearance but has a very strong, irritating odour. It exists in liquid form. It is formed by dissolving hydrogen chloride (a colourless gas) in water. As soon as the gas comes in contact with water, it sinks and mixes well with it.

A physical example of external factors affecting a process.

FUN FACT

Hydrochloric acid is sometimes called the "workhouse" chemical because of its many applications. It is used to make various products like batteries and fireworks. It is also used in the processes that make sugar and gelatin.

Order of Reaction

Changing the concentration of the reactants usually changes the rate of the reaction. A rate equation shows this effect mathematically. The order of reaction is a part of the rate equation. Orders of reaction are always calculated by performing experiments. One cannot deduce anything regarding the order of a reaction just by looking at the equation for the reaction.

A scientist adding a catalyst to a reaction.

Different orders of reaction

First order

If a reaction rate depends on a single reactant and the value of the exponent is one, then the reaction is said to be first order. In organic chemistry, first order reactions are the class of SN1 (nucleophilic substitution unimolecular) reactions. Another class of first order reactions are radioactive decay processes.

Second order

A second order reaction is when the overall order is two. The rate of a second order reaction may be proportional to one concentration squared or to the product of two concentrations. The second type has examples such as the class of SN2 (nucleophilic substitution bimolecular) reactions.

Pseudo-first order

If the concentration of a reactant stays constant, its concentration can be included in the rate constant, obtaining a pseudo first order rate equation. An example for pseudo first order is the hydrolysis of sucrose in acid solution.

Zero order

In zero order reactions, the reaction rate is independent of the concentration of a reactant; so that altering its concentration has no effect on the rate of the reaction. An example of zero order reaction is the biological oxidation of ethanol to acetaldehyde by the enzyme liver alcohol dehydrogenase in ethanol.

Redox Reaction

The word "redox" is made up of two words; reduction and oxidation. Redox reaction doesn't have a meaning on its own; it's a combination of oxidation and reduction process. In redox reaction, gain as well as loss of electrons occurs within substances. Oxidation and reduction reactions can occur alone too and are called half reactions, and these two half reactions combine to form one full redox reaction.

Rusted iron, oxidation of iron.

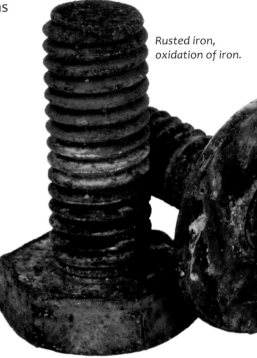

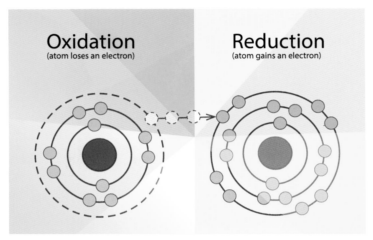

Diagrammatic representation of a redox reaction.

Redox pairs

Oxidation-reduction reactions are similar to acid-base reactions. Oxidising agents are those substances, which gain electrons and reducing agents are those substances, which lose electrons. Both oxidising and reducing agents form redox pairs.

Applications

Redox reactions are very useful in industrial processes. They are used to extract iron from the ore and also to coat the discs. For example, when we drive in our car the gasoline (which is made up of heptanes) in our car gets burned. In this reaction, the heptane atoms get oxidised and oxygen atoms are reduced. The process of photosynthesis is also an example of a redox reaction. This happens in two parts. The first part is when the oxygen present in the water that is absorbed by the plant is oxidised with the help of sunlight. The second part is where the remaining H ions from the H_2O molecules react with the carbon in the CO_2 molecules and reduce it. This is an example of a redox reaction that is carried out by the agents of nature.

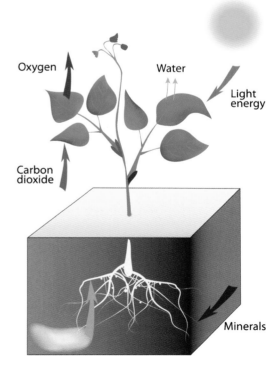

Reduction

Reduction is one half of a redox reaction. It is defined as the gain of electrons and decrease in the oxidation state. It is defined in terms of hydrogen, that is, gain of hydrogen, which is exactly the opposite of oxidation. The word reduction refers to a loss in weight, especially the loss of oxygen atoms. Reducing agents are those substances which lose electrons in a chemical reaction.

Sodium reduces silver ions to form silver.

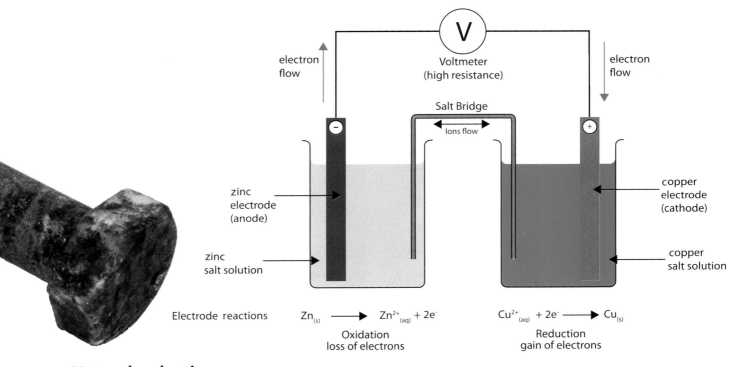

electron flow

Voltmeter (high resistance)

electron flow

Salt Bridge

Ions flow

zinc electrode (anode)

copper electrode (cathode)

zinc salt solution

copper salt solution

Electrode reactions

$Zn_{(s)} \longrightarrow Zn^{2+}_{(aq)} + 2e^-$

Oxidation
loss of electrons

$Cu^{2+}_{(aq)} + 2e^- \longrightarrow Cu_{(s)}$

Reduction
gain of electrons

Natural reduction

A simple, natural example showing oxidation process is the rusting of iron. When the iron surface reacts with the oxygen a chemical named "rust" is formed. We largely consider the rusting of any metal as oxidation and this is correct. However, the other part of this reaction is that the oxygen in the air gets reduced. This second part of the reaction counts as a reduction reaction. Chemically speaking, the oxygen atom gains electrons from the iron atoms and gets reduced.

Application

Since reduction means the gain of electrons, the major application of reduction reaction is found in the battery industry. Whether it is the little round cell that you insert in the back of your watch or the AA batteries that you put in the remote or the huge one that goes in the car, all batteries work on the principle of reduction reaction. Since the purpose of a battery is to create electricity, it works mainly by the transfer of electrons from one place to another. A battery consists of two poles, the cathode (positively charged) and the anode (negatively charged). This is surrounded by electrolyte, a liquid full of free flowing electrons. When the circuit is connected, the electrons accumulate at the anode.

Reversible Reaction

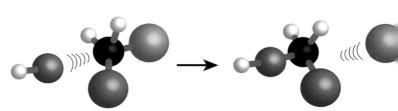

Chemical reactions form new products from the reactants. Reactions in which we are able to reverse the process and able to get the reactants back from the products are called reversible reactions. It was earlier believed that all the reactions are irreversible, but later on, with new discoveries and new concepts, it was found that it is possible to get the reactants back from the products after the chemical reaction is done.

The duality

All the reversible reactions, when written chemically, contain two arrows in the middle of the product and the reactants that face both sides. This is different than the unidirectional arrow that you will find in the middle of irreversible reactions. This type of equation shows that the reactants can't be obtained back once they have reacted with one another. The two arrows in the reversible reactions denote that even after the reaction has taken place, it is still possible for the original reactants to be obtained from it. However, they require the breaking up of the bonding forces between the atoms. In order to easily break the forces, heat energy, pressure and many other changes are introduced in the chemical reaction. This additional energy causes the molecules of the product to become unstable and break into the molecules of the reactants.

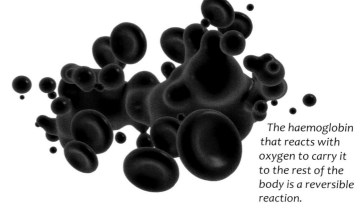

The haemoglobin that reacts with oxygen to carry it to the rest of the body is a reversible reaction.

The discovery

A scientist named Berthollet gave the concept of reversible reactions in 1803. He knew that calcium chloride and sodium carbonate react to form sodium chloride (salt) but one day, beside salt lakes, he found the formation of sodium carbonate, which was formed by the reverse reaction of the salt left after the evaporation of lake water and calcium carbonate.

Sodium carbonate deposits after the evaporation of the lake.